Mother MADE you. Mother F*CK you.

How to Identify & Avoid Toxic Men with Mommy Issues

Chanel Jasmin Clark

Copyright © 2021 by Chanel J. Clark.

All rights reserved. No part of this publication may be reproduced or transmitted in any form or by any means, electronic or mechanical, including photocopy, recording, or any information storage and retrieval system, without permission in writing from the copyright owner.

While the author has made every effort to provide accurate contact information at the time of publication, neither the author nor the publisher is responsible for errors, or for changes that occur after publication. Further, the publisher does not have any control over and does not assume any responsibility for author or third-party websites or their content.

Chanel J. Clark
PO Box 20486
New York, NY 10009

ISBN-13: 9781723839740

Printed in the United States of America

Table of Contents

INTRODUCTION 9

Chapter 1: My Personal Experience with a Toxic MIL 21

Chapter 2: The Love Triangle 53

CHAPTER 3: Emotional Incest (The Traits of a "Son-Husband") 62

CHAPTER 4: Mama's Messy Man-Child 68

CHAPTER 5: Meeting His Narcissistic Mother for the Very First Time 80

CHAPTER 6: She's Already Jealous of You ..86

Chapter 7: Her Pussy is More Powerful than Yours 92

CHAPTER 8: Hear No Evil, See No Evil......97

CHAPTER 9: Christian on Sunday…Demon During the Rest of the Week 102

Chapter 10: Cacklin' Hens 107

CHAPTER 11: Playing Both Sides of the Fence 115

CHAPTER 12: What If His Mama Is Dead?120

CHAPTER 13: Dating Tips 124

Conclusion 127

Mother MADE you.
Mother F*CK you.

Connect with SWB

www.iloveswb.com

Youtube.com/SpiritualWhistleblower

Instagram.com/SpiritualWhistleblower

TikTok/SpiritualWhistleblower

Dedication

I wanna shout out my girl Veenah. We've talked many nights about toxic mother-in-laws and sister-in-laws. Coddling a grown man only makes him weak, resentful and misogynistic. A real Queen never settles for less than what she deserves. You were built to attract a King.

God knows what He's doing. Trust Him.

Be blessed Sis.

~ Love SWB

"When I was a child, I spoke as a child, I understood as a child, I reasoned as a child: but when I became a man, I put away childish things."

— 1 Corinthians 13:11

Mother MADE you. Mother F*CK you.

How to Identify & Avoid Toxic Men with Mommy Issues

Chanel Jasmin Clark

INTRODUCTION

Phew child, let me get this out of the way RIGHT NOW! As you may know, I am a life coach who specializes in narcissistic abuse recovery. This book is based on my "various" romantic relationships, along with the stories I hear from domestic violence survivors and close acquaintances. I have too many female clients who have experienced the bullshit of a narcissistic fuckboy. When my girlfriends and I compare notes, it's always the same shit. The man starts off in love and ends up being an abusive asshole who eventually rebounds into a new relationship with the same bitch he was already cheating with during the entire relationship!

We all can come into agreement that most toxic men are raised by their controlling, narcissistic mothers who emotionally abuse their sons in order to maintain control. A narcissistic woman uses a sickening method of psychological grooming on her son called "***Trauma-bonding***." It's a process in which a female narcissist psychologically programs her son to recognize **abuse** as love. He won't even realize the extent of the damage that his mother has caused him until he starts getting into romantic relationships with women. He will repeatedly sabotage his relationships because he has misplaced anger towards his mother. In other words, you will pay the price for his bottled-up, childhood resentment.

My opinions are just that -- my opinions. You don't have to agree with me, but you do have to respect my brutal honesty. I call it for what it is. I'm tired of seeing so many good women fall victim to toxic, narcissistic men. These types of men have no backbone or direction in life because they feel that women should serve as surrogate mothers instead of significant others. They treat women like disposable Kleenex, pouncing from one relationship to the next, slanging dick and using females for their money. When this type of man is done with his victims, he will run back home to his #1 enabler: his mommy. He will retreat with his mother until he is ready to prey on and strike his next female target. He is a predator because his mommy is also a money-hungry, controlling predator.

The apple doesn't fall far from the tree. When he destroys a woman, he knows he can always go back to his mother to hide out and recharge while his victim mourns the broken transactional situationship. His mother will cover for him. This abusive cycle repeats itself over and over again, leaving behind a long trail of broken hearts and carnage. I decided that since nobody will speak up about it, I will call out the root of this destructive, misogynistic behavior for what it is. Blame his **MOTHER!**

For the women who are "empaths," motherhood can be a beautiful experience. I remember the first time I became pregnant with my daughter. I fell in love with her and I vowed to protect her and give her a better life than what my parents had given me. You see, I'm very familiar with narcissistic women because my mother is a narcissist. Everything that my mother did to abuse me, I made sure that I did the total opposite with my child. I wasn't a perfect parent, however, I made sure that my daughter never had to prove herself in order to gain my validation or approval like I had to with my mother. Growing up in an abusive, narcissistic family really changed my outlook on training up a child to be empathetic and morally grounded. My mother's abusive parenting taught me that emotional nurturing is a critical requirement in the early development years of a small child. My mother denied me the emotional bonding because she is emotionally-void.

Narcissists can emulate crocodile tears and fake empathy. There's nothing inside of their souls which is why they "mirror" the behavior of empaths in order to steal, kill and destroy their intended targets. A narcissist is nothing more than a wolf in sheep's clothing.

This constant pattern of abuse handed out by my mother, generated low self-esteem issues within myself because she was always criticizing me, well into my adult years. Nothing I ever did really impressed my mother or made her happy. I was constantly seeking her validation, albeit, she found much joy in ignoring me. My mother was flat out evil. It took me many years to figure out that she was and still is a narcissist.

I started doing research on the dynamics of narcissistic women and the relationships they have with their children. The differences in how they treat their sons from their daughters are also greatly impacted based on a variable of factors. I also paid close attention to how my mother treated my younger brother and this was another contributing factor as to why I decided to write this book. So I've applied all of this information and research on narcissistic men and I found a pattern. Broken men who were raised by broken women, go out into the world and create more broken victims. It's a sick, dysfunctional cycle.

I've dated my share of fuckboys and it literally took me *all the way* out. I couldn't figure out for the life of me what I was doing wrong. I became the perfect girlfriend and wife for a plethora of toxic men who didn't really know how to receive my type of love. I used to blame myself for *THEIR* abusive behaviors. I would overwork myself to try and get it right. I became every narcissist's surrogate mommy, jumping through hoops to please their ungrateful, self-entitled asses. It absolutely got me nowhere. The more I gave, the more I would end up depleted and destroyed. I stopped dating for a long time to do some soul searching to figure out why I was attracting these horrible types of men and the answers stem from the trauma bond I have with my mother. I was dating men who had the same personality as my narcissistic parents.

Fuckboys are like a bewildered species right? You can't help but to stare at them in sheer amazement. Almost like watching a deer leap across the highway in front of your car. The audacity of these creatures! So bold and so daring.

When that deer jumps out in front of your car and stares at you in shock before he collides with the windshield, it's almost as if he's reading your mind and sending telepathic messages, lol. *"I'm a deer and I can do what I want, how I want it. Now I dare you to hit me. If you hit me, I'll do a lot of damage to your car!"* This is the mentality of a fuckboy. He has self-entitlement issues and he will blatantly overstep your personal boundaries. Always displaying risky, above-the-law behavior without a single care or regard for how his actions will affect those around him.

Well, it's sad to say this but, we have an ongoing epidemic of fuckboys multiplying within this generation. I mean, there have always been the typical bad boys and players who eventually grow up to be responsible husbands after they stop playing the field, however, the fuckboy is a new rare breed of species, lol. The fuckboy is flat out a narcissist. A delusional, arrogant, haughty, disrespectful, promiscuous, brazen, manipulative, lying, deceitful, gossiping, spoiled five year old child, trapped inside of an adult male body. Listen, I'm done with fuckboys! I had a good run in my younger whore days and I refuse to deal with that shit anymore. The constant lies, cheating, self-entitled passive/aggressiveness of an oversized toddler, is played the fuck out! **I'M COMPLETELY OVER IT**!

More importantly, I'm tired of seeing "elderly" trifling women who cripple and coddle their sons so that their sons can be useless to any woman who wants to have a healthy relationship with them. Yes, these types of toxic women set their sons up for relationship failure when they become men.

You want to know when this madness will end? I will tell you when it will end. When women stop treating their sons like their boyfriends/ husbands. When women stop enabling their sons to commit domestic violence against their girlfriends/ wives. When women stop trying to control their sons for fear that their sons will get married to a better quality woman. When women stop physically assaulting and molesting their sons and sweeping the abuse underneath the rug. When women stop allowing their husbands and boyfriends to molest their young boys. When women learn to heal before allowing broken men access into their lives. Women, please WAKE UP! We are just as accountable as the sorry ass men who deliberately target us. Everyone must be held accountable!

Until these issues are addressed accordingly, we will continue to see an influx of fuckboys degrade and disrespect our daughters. Even the good girls who were raised by strong men can get conned into a relationship with a narcissist, so nobody is safe these days.

Shame on you narcissistic mothers for being the toxic enablers that you are! Spoiling your son instead of teaching him how to work hard for his rewards. Buying him a new pair of Jordans every month, instead of teaching him how to value the ones he already has. Your son lacks boundaries! Shame on you for allowing your big ass baby boy to continue to sleep in the bed with you so he feels more like your boyfriend instead of your son.

Shame on you for allowing him to get away with bullying someone else's child! Women are the root of a narcissist's bad behavior towards females. Let's deal with the truth. Read on.

If you're offended by anything you've just read, then you are definitely a big part of the problem. Our men are failing us because they are being groomed to be controlled and destroyed by women. If he can't trust the woman who gave birth to him, he will punish all women for her mistakes. Emotional incest is a generational curse. The cycle must be broken.

Mother MADE you.
Mother F*CK you.

Chapter 1: My Personal Experience with a Toxic MIL

I am going to change the names in my story, but this is based on *my truth* and I'm gonna tell it how it's supposed be told: truthfully. I had a high school male friend (*let's call him Trash Boy, lol*), who has a toxic mother who assisted him with playing me behind my back. His mother was a messy, promiscuous, financially-abusive, fake church-going, nosey, two-faced, coddling ass woman who meddled in her son's private life 24/7. She knew he abused women because she was an abused woman. When he was a little boy, his father beat his mother, so in their household, domestic violence was considered normal behavior.

Me and "*Trash Boy*" were good friends and lived in the same neighborhood in South Carolina.

He was a star athlete who played football and basketball with my brother. He was very popular in high school. We graduated together and then I left to go on to college in 1994 to Louisiana and never returned back (*until he summoned me to come back 25 years later*).

During the time I was away at college, I graduated and ventured off to New York City. I became very successful and secured a modeling career. I worked my way around the music industry as well because I majored in Broadcast Journalism and Mass Communications.

More than 15 years after, an old friend from high school contacted me via Facebook and mentioned to me that "*Trash Boy*" had been locked up in federal prison for 20 years. I was in shock, so I looked up *Trash Boy's* sister to get his address to write him and see how he was doing. I hadn't seen or heard from him since 1993. I wrote him after he had served his first ten years. At the time I was married, so I wasn't looking to flirt, rather I only wanted to check up on him and find out exactly what had happened because I had heard so many negative rumors. Based on our friendship and what I remembered about him, I found it hard to believe that he had committed these crimes. He had never showed me a criminal side to him at all. I had to hear it from him in order to believe it. I was almost certain that he would have gone to the NFL or NBA. He had a promising future career in professional sports, so to learn that he threw his whole life away, was disheartening to say the least.

We exchanged a few letters and chatted on the phone a few times, nothing more, nothing less. My letters to him were very platonic, wishing him well. I didn't send him any money, nor did I give him the impression that I wanted anything romantic. I just wanted to hear directly from him what had happened and to wish him well.

He wanted to continue writing me, however, I wanted to move on. After all, he was the cocky, arrogant high school football player and star athlete that I remembered from high school. He was used to girls chasing him and throwing themselves at him. I wasn't that type of girl and besides I would never violate my husband like that. After we exchanged a couple of letters, I cut ties.

He continued to try to maintain contact with me, but I ignored his prison letters and went on about my life. It wasn't until another nine years had gone by that he had been released from prison. He had his sister hunt me down on Facebook to get my number to get in touch with him. She told me he was looking for me so I gave her my number. I was also divorced from my husband and single, so I felt there wasn't any harm in reconnecting with him. Let me just clarify.

He got in touch with me immediately. He had been released into a halfway house post his prison release. We talked morning, noon and night on the phone. We texted each other non-stop. When we spoke, he sounded like he had gave his life over to the Lord and had turned over a new leaf (*it was a bunch of bullshit*). Our connection was incredibly strong. He had me mentally hooked and he started pouring out his heart and his feelings he claimed that he always had for me. He said he had to see me again. I don't know what drew me closer to him after 20+ years, but I wanted to believe that he was a man of God. I wanted to believe that he had gotten his mind, body and spirit right while he was incarcerated over those 20 years. I wanted to ignore the negative rumors I had heard about him. Besides, he had never hurt me or did anything bad to me. We were honestly great friends and I never saw a bad side to him. I believe in giving everyone a fair chance until proven guilty otherwise.

He convinced me to move out of state to live with him permanently (*with the end goal of us getting married*) because I immediately asked him what his intentions were. He told me that he had to serve three months in the halfway house and then he was going to be paroled to his mother's house. He wanted me to leave NYC to move with him in his mom's home. I wasn't comfortable with that, but he assured me that if I moved in with him, we would be moved out within three months (**HUGE MISTAKE**).

When we finally met up, it was a crazy attraction that was unexplainable. We had amazing sex and were inseparable. I didn't realize at the time, he was love-bombing me. I had gone back to New York City after visiting with him for a weekend and I couldn't stop thinking about him. We continued to call each other non-stop. We were like two young teenagers talking all day and night.

We couldn't miss a day without hearing from each other. We had the best conversations and talked about everything. Whatever was going on in the world, the news, the streets or wherever, we talked deeply about it. If we missed each other's phone calls, it felt strange. We were bonded, even after not seeing each other for 25 years, we had become inseparable. I honestly loved him.

After some time had passed, we longed for each other and I could not do the long distance relationship thing any longer. I had done it before with other men and it didn't last long. *"Trash Boy"* convinced me to move 705 miles down south to be with him. He was paroled to his mama's house and that's where I fucked up and should have waited before moving. I should have waited until he got his shit together. He didn't have his own place and car, yet I allowed him to pressure me to move in with him at his raggedy mama's house. I ignored my intuition and trusted his words too much and ended up getting burned. I totally hold myself accountable.

Initially, our plan was to save up some money for a few months and move into a one bedroom apartment. I have always been independent, so I didn't feel right living in his mother's home. I've always had my own shit and I don't depend on nobody for nothing. It felt weird, but I trusted him to lead me. I was submissive and wanted to see nothing but the good in him. I had faith that everything would turn out okay. So I found a good job, prepared to move in with him and that's when his true colors came out.

For a little while, we were getting along great, having sex 3 times a day, every single day. Our chemistry was off the hook. We spent every day, all day together. We were inseparable. I would drop him off to work, cook him breakfast, pack his lunch, pick him up after work and make sure his dinner was cooked. I was his in-house wife (*more like in-house slave*). We would go to the gym together to work out every day. We would go grocery shopping, you name it. We were always together. I was more like his homie at some point, drinking and smoking with him, listening to good music on the weekends. Taking long drives and going to the beach. I was too caught up in my feelings to realize that he was actually grooming me and preparing to abuse me behind closed doors. He was softening me up for the kill.

One day, he invited me to go with him to his family reunion. Since he did not have a car nor did his mother, I provided the transportation (*they both took full advantage of that too*). We went to the family reunion and he introduced me to all of his relatives as his fiancé. We had a great time. He wanted me to get up and dance with him, but I did not feel comfortable doing so at the time because I wanted him to bond with his "adult" daughter (*they had fallen out at the time and were just mending their relationship*). I didn't want to give his daughter the impression that I was trying to steal her father from her, so I respectfully bowed out and stayed classy. I encouraged him to talk to his daughter, eat with her and dance with her. I had no idea that I was going to pay a hefty price for trying to do something right.

After the family reunion was over, we got into my car to go home and about a mile down the road, he started to rage and cuss at me! He goes off on me, yelling from the top of his lungs about how I embarrassed him. I looked at him in disbelief and I said, "What are you talking about? How did I embarrass you?" He said, "***You wouldn't dance with me in front of my family!***" My mouth just dropped open in utter disbelief.

He cussed me out all the way home (*and it was a long country ride home, might I add*). My nerves were totally all over the place and my anxiety was way up. He had taken a minor incident and treated it as if I had cheated on him. His anger issues were now being exposed to me. I couldn't believe my long-time friend from high school was behaving like this. I had never seen this side of him. I was in total shock.

From that point on, he began ranting more and more behind closed doors. He turned into this monster and became verbally abusive. He looked like a demon who couldn't contain his emotions whenever he didn't get his way. A giant toddler who felt entitled to have it his way all of the time. Screaming, yelling and demanding respect from those closest to him, yet refusing to respect others in return. He isolated me from my friends and family, so I began to drink alcohol more. I grew depressed because he constantly had me walking on eggshells.

He was depriving me of sleep in the middle of the night in order to start arguments of false accusations of cheating. I never cheated on this man, but he was paranoid all of the time! I was completely depleted every day when it came time to get up and start my day because he worked my last fuckin nerve! I was DRAINED.

It wasn't until one day that I had gotten fed up of his verbal abuse and name calling, that I decided it was time to pack my shit and leave. I was wearing my eye glasses at the time and I went to grab a bunch of my belongings along with my car keys. He went back and forth with his rants. One minute he would yell at me and tell me to get the fuck out, then he would recant his statement and beg me to stay. It was an emotional rollercoaster, but I was making my first attempt to leave him. I had a handful of clothes and toiletries in my hand. I was headed to the front door and he blocked me. He stood in front of the door and looked me directly in the eye. He asked me, "***Where the fuck do you think you're going?***" I told him it was time for me to go. I'm trying to de-escalate a potentially nasty argument.

I hate confrontations and I hate dealing with people at all. He knew this about me. He knew I was an introvert who was peaceful at heart. I was not in a position to fight him or challenge him, I just wanted to go! Next thing you know, he takes his index finger and knocks my glasses off of my face, body slams me down to the ground. My personal possessions were all over the living room floor. My head almost hit the corner of his mother's glass coffee table. He had knocked me down swiftly with extreme force. My head hit the hard wood floor and then it happened...

He put his hands around my neck and began choking me to the point my vision started to blur. He had no shirt on and was very sweaty. I couldn't grab him because my hands kept slipping off of his slimy body. I tried to push him off of me, but he was incredibly strong. He kept ramming my head onto the floor over and over again. I cried from the pain and I struggled to breathe. I thought I was going to die.

He let up off of me, then I rolled over on my side into a fetal position and he began kicking me repeatedly in the back of the head and all over my back and rib cage. I thought he would never stop beating me. It felt like a torturous ongoing assault from the man whom I thought loved me. At that very moment, he treated me like an inmate locked up in a caged cell. He had blacked out and fought me like a man. He thought he was in prison when he put his hands on me. I never looked at him the same ever again, but I couldn't bring myself to leave him despite the abuse. I was trauma-bonded.

He said, "**Shut the fuck up and get up or else I will give you something to cry about**!" I had a mouth full of blood because when he knocked me down to the ground, my teeth punctured my gums and inner mouth. He threatened to beat me up some more if I didn't stop crying. I ran to the bathroom and spit up blood in the sink. I looked in the mirror at the bruises all over my shoulders.

He told me to get in the shower and clean myself up. I cried in the shower and he threatened me again. So I had to cry in silence. Once I finished washing up, he demanded that I go to bed with him. I couldn't leave if I'd try. He had confiscated my car keys, my clothes, my laptop and my purse. Basically, I was being held captive against my will.

When we laid down to go to bed, he told me to pray with him, but I was totally numb and couldn't say a word. He held my hand and he asked God to forgive him for what he had done to me. I started to cry again. He then got on top of me and he penetrated me; we began to have sex without my consent. I damn sure wasn't in the mood. I was actually disgusted and I wasn't sexually attracted to him anymore. Unfortunately, I didn't have a choice, he took it from me and I had to comply. I couldn't run anywhere, I had no place to go. I was isolated from my friends and family. Where could I go? I felt defeated. At that point, I realized that I had been set up to be his personal servant and I was trapped. This was all a calculated plot to trick me into moving in with him so that he could break me down to nothing and control me. He was repeating the same abuse cycle that he saw his father do to his mother. Isolate, assault and control.

These beatings and his awful outbursts continued for as long as I could tolerate them. I even witnessed him on two occasions, threatened to hit his own mother in front of me. He cussed his mother out on a regular basis for keeping her house filthy as well as her being a manipulative user, liar and whore who spent her nights sleeping with different men for favors. He talked to his mother like she was a dog. I should have left the moment I saw him do it the first time because the reality is, men who talk to their mothers like shit, will talk to ALL women like shit. And that's exactly what happened, he eventually started talking to me like he talks to his mother.

Now here comes the fun part: his baby mothers. He had two women who he got pregnant around the same time after we graduated high school twenty years ago. Both of his kids are about a year apart in age; they're adults now. Simultaneously, he had gotten one woman pregnant, and the other one pregnant right after. He then triangulated both women and had them disliking each other, fighting over him for years. He told me several stories about both women, making fun of them and calling them both derogative names and criticizing their parenting skills. He referred to both women as obsessive and crazy. Looking back, I know he probably dogged me out to both women as well because he's the type of man to start drama and sit back while females fight over him. He did this to boost his own ego, but I never fell for it. I'm too beautiful and too successful to envy either women who I clearly feel are **NOT** on my level. He tried it though.

He would try to make me jealous during our relationship by telling me that each baby mama would text him late at night to flirt with him. I now realize that he told me these stories only to make me feel insecure and competitive of both baby mothers. He did all of that to get an emotional reaction out of me.

Truth be told, I'm sure he talked badly about me, to both of them. This is the game of a true narcissistic sociopath. Staging catfights between the women in his life, then sitting back and eating popcorn with a smirk on his face, watching the drama unfold.

To make a long story short, he was living a double life screwing one of his baby mamas behind my back and his mother knew all about it. We were living together in his mother's house, saving money to move into our own apartment while he was cheating on me and giving me Bacterial Vaginosis from creeping on his lunch breaks with his babymother. His mother witnessed the beatings, assault, abuse and cheating he did to me and still protected him by sweeping his dirt underneath the rug and assisting his babymother with removing me out of the picture. His mother is a fuckin covert narcissist. A piece of shit scumbag ass bitch. Pure trash. A demon with a dress on.

Another factor. If his kids are grown, why is he still sleeping with his baby mama behind my back?

What is she calling and texting for? She damn sure ain't calling for diaper money or child support. I later learned that she popped up to his mother's house while we were at work. She felt compelled to hold a conversation with his mother in regards to pressuring him to move in with her. He was trying to get his residency transferred to her house with his probation officer (*This all came out in the end when I called his probation officer and she gave me the real tea on his plans to move in with his baby mother*). I guess his mother wanted him out of her house because she was sick of his verbal abuse, and since she was already familiar with his baby mother, they ALL decided to work together to erase me out of the picture.

This way his mother could kick him out of her house by pushing him to move in with his baby mother and send me packing back to New York. He hated his mother's dirty house too and apparently his baby mother is a narcissistic doormat who always provided him with money (*a dumb ass sugar mama*). So it all made sense for everyone to work together underhandedly to kick me out of the family. I wasn't a Sugarmama or doormat. But instead of them kicking me out, he started arguments to put me in a position to break things off ***first*** so that he wouldn't come off as looking like the bad guy. This would allow him to get off Scott-free with rebounding into a new relationship with his babymother while his toxic family pretended like me and him were never in a relationship. The family could sweep his dirt underneath the rug and live happily ever after. The way that this shit went down was foul because his mother AND his babymother are narcissists. They've done this with other women before, so it came easy when it was time to **PLOT** against me.

    I still blame my ex for entertaining the bait. All he ever did was complain to me about how miserable his babymother was and how she wanted to control him and make him just as miserable. I don't believe him 100% because I'm sure he blew smoke up her ass and gossiped about me negatively to her in order to get back into her life, playing both of us against each other. He probably told her that he wanted his family back and to be with her and his son like the old days, so they both plotted to get me out of the picture. The fucked up shit was that his mother and sister were also in on the gig. Everybody knew that I was being played behind my back except for me. The whole family is sneaky and fake. I blame all of them for playing a role in enabling his abusive behavior and cheating.

Anyhow, he claimed that his babymother was pressuring him to get back with her right around the time he and I had applied for our marriage license application. He had taken me out to go shopping for my engagement ring. He told me that his babymother was lurking in the shadows, trying to break us up.

The plan was for us to pick up our marriage license and get married on my birthday, but as my birthday got closer, he started to act funny and "gaslight" me. He was playing mind games and staging arguments between me and his other family members (*Triangulation*). He knows I'm a ticking time bomb and I will go off if anyone plays with my emotions.

I'm so thankful to be out of that situation and I don't want to be associated or affiliated with that family ever again. I'm grateful that I didn't get pregnant or married. The blessing was in the betrayal.

At the end of the day, I caught him and the babymother creeping together 2 days before my birthday. Go figure. He had his alibi together. He had a motive to stage a break up in order to have a reason to sleep with her despite our plans to fly to New York for my birthday.

Despite our plans to get married on my birthday. Despite the fact that he has asked me to put up with his bullshit, his verbal and physical assaults and to **not** report him to his probation officer for domestic violence. Despite everything that this motherfucker had put me through during our relationship, he begged me to stay and work things out. He didn't want me to quit on him and he wanted me to continue to have this incredible amount of patience with him because he's still adapting to his freedom from prison life.

Crazy though, the moment he gets an opportunity to cheat on me with his low hanging fruit, low self-esteem ass baby mother, he sabotages everything we had. He actually thought that I was going to stick around and let him get away with his shenanigans. Listen, **I WAS DONE**! I kicked his sorry ass to the curb, changed my cell phone number. Completely blocked his entire family from contacting me. His mama, sister, you name it... **#BLOCKT**! I didn't want none of his family contacting me or keeping tabs on me, now or ever again. After I broke things off, he had the nerve to run a smear campaign telling everyone I was stalking him when he was the one stalking me, calling my job after I changed my cell number. I didn't want his dirty dick, yuck mouth, broke, **DELUSIONAL** ass no more. His baby mother actually did me a huge favor. She collected my trashy sloppy seconds so I could be free to start living my life again. Game over!

So where does his toxic mother come in to play? Well the entire time we was living together (*in her house*), she witnessed him beat on me. She witnessed the violence, verbal abuse and blatant disrespect towards me. Not only that, he was incredibly disrespectful towards her. Called her all types of "Bitches" and told her she kept a dirty house. Yelled at her for smoking weed all of the time; for being promiscuous. He used to talk to her like shit every single day. That should have been a big red flag for me because anytime a man disrespects his mother, it only means that he will never respect any other woman that comes into his life, whether it be his wife, girlfriend or daughter. He is a Misogynist to the core, no thanks to his toxic mother enabling his trifling behavior!

Anyway, at the time that I moved into her house, I saw that he was sleeping on her couch because he did not have a bed to sleep in. She has a 4 bedroom house and her bedroom was the only room that contained a mattress in it. So I went out and purchased a new mattress so that we could sleep comfortably. Her house was also hot, so I purchased an air conditioner. I had no problem doing so because I'm the kind of person that loves to help people. I respected his mother and appreciated the fact that she had accepted me into her home because she saw that I genuinely loved her son and wanted to help him get back on his feet.

She didn't have a car and he didn't have a car, so I provided them with transportation and drove them everywhere. I kept groceries in the refrigerator. Constantly did favors. They both took advantage. Both of them are liars, users and con artists. I'm glad that God removed me from that toxic environment before my real monetary blessings came in. I realize now that had I still been dealing with both of them today, they would have felt entitled to taking more of my money from me now that I'm running my own lucrative business. It's funny how God has blessed me with a six-figure income as an entrepreneur, now that I leveled up after leaving my ex and his trifling family!

I saw his mother as a church-going Christian with a good heart in the very beginning, but as I started figuring out that her son was a lying, cheating, manipulative scum bag and she was fully aware of his bullshit, I started to look at her differently. I lost a lot of respect for his mother and saw her as weak. I also saw a pattern of passive-aggressive behavior from her, which is where her son gets his hot/cold behavior from. He hated her because he behaved just like her and had so many of her trifling ways. It's unfortunate that he is not mature enough to break the dysfunction he grew up around. He wasn't strong enough to cut permanent ties with both of his abusive parents to build a new life with me. I feel sorry for the woman after me.

I cannot be in a relationship with a man who stays connected to the toxicity of his dysfunctional family. In his eyes it was cool for him to gossip about his family to me, but he also would flip sides when we had our arguments and sit up with his toxic family to gossip about me. He played both sides of the fence along with his mother and sister. He behaved like the toxic women he grew up around and didn't know how to break free from it. I now realize that he tried to break me down behind closed doors so that I could be weak-minded, toxic and messy like his mother, sister and both of his baby mothers.

The women in his family are narcissists, which is why he chose to impregnate both of his baby mothers. He recycled and passed down the toxicity he learned from his mother, by getting two female narcissists pregnant to continue the dysfunction in his family. One nasty, toxic, ongoing cycle of dysfunctional trash. I wasn't having it. I'm not like none of the bitches in his family, which is why I will NEVER water myself down or kiss nobody's ass to fit in. Fuck him and all of those bitches! I don't affiliate with trash. That's the type of women he will constantly be attracted to, and I'm not that type. I couldn't deal with that toxic shit no more. I was depressed and had to break free from it, so I moved back to New York.

When I dumped him, I moved out of his mother's house and took all of my belongings. I called her and she kept telling me that she apologizes for everything. She could feel my pain after I told her I caught her son creeping with his weak, recycled-doormat, toxic ass baby mama. His mother knew I was hurt, but the painful truth was, she had already knew ahead of time that the game was rigged against me from day one.

His mama is the same woman who begged me to continue to stay with her son after she saw the bruises he put all over my body. This is the same woman who begged me not to retaliate against her son, but she knew he was dogging me behind my back. This is the same woman who claims she is strong, but is more concerned with protecting her son's deplorable, misogynistic behavior towards females, including herself. She was his #1 enabler and it all came out at the very end. I had lost all respect for her. Period. Point blank.

As the drama unfolded and I got my shit and got the fuck out of that toxic environment, I paid his mother my final rent, placed the house keys on his bed. I called her and told her I was coming to pick up my mattress with a van. You wanna know what that bitch said? *"I don't know Chanel, that mattress looks good in my house. I gotta think about it and I will get back to you!"*

What the fuck? I was still making payments on the bed and I have all of my receipts! How is this bitch going to keep my bed, knowing I'm homeless, crippled and grieving, going through a heart break? Hello Bitch, I'm homeless. Give me my motherfucking bed! Your son is sleeping in another woman's bed, but you want to continue to hold on to the mattress knowing I paid for it? She knows her son lied, cheated and assaulted me, so she wants to add insult to injury by holding on to my property. So basically, I have to shop for a new mattress when I move into my new apartment is what she's saying? **BITCH FUCK YOU AND YOUR TRIFLING SON!**

At that point, I WAS REALLY DONE! No, I mean DONE, DONE! My ex wasn't the only toxic individual in that household. His mother definitely was. I thought his fake-Christian-church-going mother was stronger than that. Apparently, she enjoys the drama because she inserted herself right in the middle of it. She is going to continue to enable her son to abuse women. She is going to continue to allow her son to verbally disrespect her in her own house. She is going to continue to sweep everything under the rug. This is why her son scams, manipulates, uses people and takes advantage of women... he learned it from his mammie! Like mother, like son!

I hope you have learned something from this story. When toxic women teach their sons that abuse equates love, their sons will go out into the world and continue to abuse other women.

The first woman that a man connects with is his mother. She gives birth to him and nurses him from her breast. She is the first woman he makes physical contact with. She is the first woman he sees naked and undressed. She is the first woman that he watches his father kiss and touch.

He learns everything about a woman, from his **MOTHER**. She sets the initial standard for her son to follow when it comes to choosing a woman. If his mother is toxic, he will seek to settle or impregnate TOXIC women because he's addicted to drama. Sure he will want to be seen with a high quality, self-respecting woman, but the woman he "settles with" will nine times out of ten, be a toxic piece of shit like his mother (*hence why he runs back to his toxic babymother, toxic ex-wife or side chick*).

He needs to always have a narcissistic tramp by his side to coddle and enable his fuckery. A quality woman with high standards won't stick around or entertain that shit. He will constantly break up with women who hold high standards only to run back to the downgraded babymama and/or ratchet ass hood rats that he can walk all over because his mother embodies the same characteristics. This is what he grew up around, so this is what he will forever be accustomed to settling for. He loves toxic bitches because his mommy is toxic!

Please note. If this whore (*his mama*) has led a piss poor example of what an outstanding Queen should be in front of her son, he's already ruined. If she is weak and allows men to disrespect her in front of her son, he's already ruined. If she is a whore who sleeps with multiple men in front of her son, he's already ruined. If she neglects her son emotionally, he's already ruined. If she physically assaults or molests her son or allows another man to abuse her son, he's already ruined. If she puts another man before her son, he's already ruined. If she treats her son as if he's her husband instead of her child, guess what? You guessed it. He's already ruined! His mother is **Narcissist**!

These are the women who are breeding and raising narcissistic fuckboys! Society is quick to blame the absent father when a child is raised by a single mother, but contrary to popular belief, an abusive woman will destroy her son and groom him to stay close to home before he becomes an adult.

By the time he becomes a man, she has already ruined him, so he's no good in any relationship with any high quality, self-respecting woman. This psycho ass bitch has raised a boy into a GROWN BOY. He is allowed to stray and even get married, but his mother has trained him to sabotage his relationships to run back home to her because in her eyes, she owns him. His mother thinks he is her personal property not to be shared with any other woman unless she can control that woman (*Hence, an obedient, doormat daughter-in-law*). His mother is a covert narcissist. Please abandon and block his **ENTIRE** family once you see that you are being manipulated.

Mother MADE you.
Mother F*CK you.

Chapter 2: The Love Triangle

Ladies, when you get into a relationship with a narcissistic man, you have yet to find out that you are involved in a toxic love triangle and no I'm not talking about the love triangle with his side chick. Pay attention because this shit gets deep. If your man is truly a narcissist, sociopath or psychopath, then you're gonna learn in the end that his mother is his "**original**" side chick. She is his *permanent* side chick and always will be throughout the duration of all of his failed romantic relationships.

How does a narcissistic mother turn her son out and become his devoted mistress? Well, because she is a narcissist, her son has been enduring emotional abuse from the time he was a child. As his mother, she is going to deny him the emotional development that is required in order for a boy to process healthy emotions as a mature man. She reinforces her authority over her son's life until he is strong enough to scare her into submission. He achieves this once he becomes a teenager and she can no longer beat him or threaten him with dominance. But it's too late because by the time he grows to become physically stronger in his teens, the emotional damage has been done.

She has programmed her son through a process called "reinforced intermittence." This is a psychological conditioning process where she (*or his abusive father*) assaults her son and then coddles him by telling him it's love. One minute he hates her for abusing him but then he loves her because he is being groomed to never betray her despite her ongoing abuse tactics. This creates a trauma bond that will forever connect her son to her energetically, even if he ventures out into the world and gets married. He has been programmed to always return back to his abusive mother so that she can relinquish her control over him, even as a grown man with a wife and kids.

The outcome of his mother abusing him in this manner can have two different results. You have to understand as well that abuse is not always physical. His narcissistic mother can emasculate, taunt and financially abuse her son. She can have multiple relationships with men in front of her son. These are all different forms of emotional, traumatic abuse at the behest of a narcissistic mother. All of these abuse tactics will have a permanent negative impact on any young boy and his view on all women.

A male that is raised by a woman like this can either turn into a full blown narcissist himself, or he will either eternally cut his mother off when he flees from her grasp by moving far away from her. Once he escapes her clutches, he will commit to breaking the cycle of dysfunction that she taught him as a child. He will go on to marry a good woman with high standards, whose qualities are the complete opposite of his toxic mother. He will then proceed to build a new life with his beautiful wife and kids minus the abuse that he was exposed to when he was a child. He is committed to breaking the generational curse because his mother has traumatized him to the point of no return. He knows that his relationship with his toxic mother will suffer of course, but he doesn't care because severing ties with her abusive control is worth it.

A man who turns into a narcissist as a result of his mother teaching him emotional manipulation, will repeat what his mommy taught him as he becomes an adult and go out into the world to prey on multiple good women to entrap them for further devaluation. The women he chooses to bring home to meet his mother are unknowing victims who are inadvertently caught in a spider web of emotional destruction. His mother has programmed him to facilitate an abusive love triangle which consists of herself, her son and his new victim (*you*). The toxic love triangle ensures that both she and her son receive narcissistic supply from you before replacing you with the side chick waiting next in line. The love triangle secures each victim in place. (***please see illustration***):

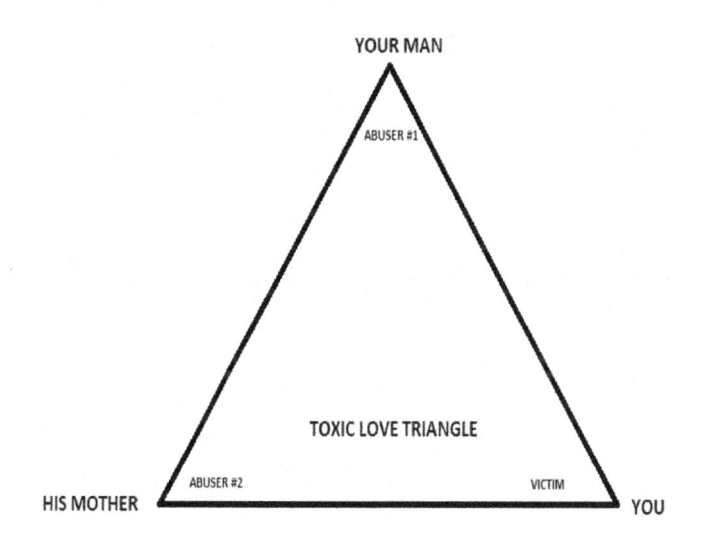

```
              YOUR MAN
                 /\
                /  \
               /ABUSER #1
              /      \
             /        \
            /          \
           /            \
          /              \
         /                \
        /                  \
       /  TOXIC LOVE TRIANGLE\
      /                      \
     / ABUSER #2        VICTIM \
HIS MOTHER ─────────────────── YOU
```

As the illustration depicts, your man and his mother are the two abusers in this sick twisted scenario. They are both narcissists, however, at this early point in the relationship, you aren't aware of it. They both have to go through a process where they seduce you first to get you comfortable and locked in before they both tag team against you to initiate the abuse cycle.

They will both use an abuse tactic called "Triangulation" where one will play you against the other. When you and him have arguments, he will run to his mother and gossip negatively about you to her. If he has a nasty confrontation with his mother, he will run to you and gossip about his mother. If his mother gets tired of his bullying, she will call you on the phone and talk shit about her own son to you. This is all **Triangulation**. The art of staging cat fights and playing people against each other. Don't get caught up in their drama because they will turn on each other, but come back together again to team up against you if it benefits them.

His mother is a pimp living vicariously through her son. If both of them can work together to lock down a good woman with a secure job, then they both have hit jackpot because they both plan on using you. Her son must bring you to meet her to get her approval. When you think she's being nice to you, she's really screening you for your vulnerabilities because she is plotting, along with her son, to use you financially. She is also fully aware of all of the other women that her son is cheating with behind your back. He will use his mother or his toxic sister to help him carry out the cheating and deception. This is why when you find out in the end that your man is being unfaithful, you're also gonna learn that his entire family knew the side chicks all along. They all will smile in your face but kick it with the side chick when you're not around. Fuckin snakes.

The family is all narcissistic and they move together like demons in order to enable your lover to keep securing narcissistic supply. It's a really sick way of manipulating and discarding good people like trash for personal/ financial gain. Before you learn about the side chick, you will also learn that his mama is subconsciously running his life like an obsessed puppet master. He told you he hates his mother, but the truth is, he can't live his life without her because she enables his toxicity.

Remember, she's been programming him to be her son-husband from the time he was born. He's already ruined. You're just a pawn in the game that is being pimped out for your assets and resources. She sends her son out into the world to prey on the innocent like a lion scoping out a zebra. Once the lion makes the kill, he will share the zebra with his family to feast together. You get the picture? Good. His mother is the ring leader. She taught her son the trick of the trade. When you break up with him, make sure you block his entire family. They are all sick, dysfunctional, manipulative opportunists and users. Remove yourself from the demonic love triangle. They are both running game on you.

Mother MADE you.
Mother F*CK you.

CHAPTER 3: Emotional Incest (*The Traits of a "Son-Husband"*)

The narcissistic mother loves to keep her titties in her grown boy's mouth. She will allow him to nurse from her breast until he's old and gray. If he is her only son, she will groom him to be her love child and demon child. If she has more than one son, she will choose one boy as her favorite (*the golden child*), and the other boy to bully and abuse (*the scapegoat child*). Her parenting skills are those of a dictator. She lacks nurturing skills and emotional bonding that is required to build and develop a child emotionally in their early stages; the very important thing that every child needs during their most critical time in early childhood. Either way, all children involved are being abused.

Unfortunately, there is a serious lack of fathers because narcissistic/sociopathic men abandon their parental responsibilities to seek out new victims to impregnate and use. Single parent homes are skyrocketing through the roof. It is now an epidemic in the United States; a constant pattern of irresponsibility and unaccountability, unfairly dumped onto our children who eventually end up paying the price derived from toxic parenting.

It's amazing how the absence of a father can affect children. The devastating impact that it can have on both genders will only play out later in the child's adult romantic relationships with the opposite sex. A little girl will grow up seeking validation from every toxic man she sleeps with because she yearns for a father-figure or she'll either become a predatory gold-digger thanks to her narcissistic mother.

But what about a little boy? What will he become as a result of being raised by a single woman who's narcissistic? The absence of a father in a young boy's life is very profound. The boy is in dire need of leadership skills; things that only a real man can teach him. He needs a father to teach him how to lead, provide and protect for his family when he becomes a man.

A father is supposed to show his son how to treat women with respect and dignity. He needs his father to lead by example. If his father abuses women, abandons his responsibilities and lacks leadership qualities, then his son is left to learn from the men in his family or his mother.

The unfortunate scenario is that a single mother who is toxic and narcissistic, will do more damage to her son than any absent father could ever do. She is a very sick, demented bitch, who will invoke emotional incest on her son and treat him more like a lover instead of an offspring.

The dynamics between a narcissistic mother and her son are much different from that of her daughter. When she gives birth to a boy, she takes on a mother/wife role. She gets total gratification knowing her son is under her total control. He's dependent on her as a child and she loves to feel needed. This provides her with narcissistic supply. When people think she is nurturing her baby, she's actually emotionally feeding off of her child like a parasite. She oozes over the compliments that people give her when they tell her how cute her baby boy is. She sops up the narcissistic supply every time she posts photos of her son on social media and people like/comment under her pics. Her son is the gateway to fulfilling her bottomless self-esteem. She's grooming him from infancy. Yes, the abuse starts from the moment she pushes the boy out of her womb.

The narcissistic mother uses her baby boy/grown son as a crutch to sustain her low self-esteem. As he becomes older, she will selfishly reinforce her control over her son to make sure he never strays from her side. He doesn't realize that he has now become an extension of his toxic mother instead of becoming his own individual self. She's not going to allow him to create his own identity because she has no identity. Her control issues will go into overdrive and the process of training her boy to stay stuck to her hip despite her abusive tactics will be ongoing into his adulthood. To put it plainly, this is one sick, insecure bitch with a plan to set out to destroy anyone who can possibly put an emotional hold on her son. She is the only one with that type of power and she will wield it in any woman's face. Her son will suffer repeatedly and he will learn to adapt to it. He will never heal and that's exactly how she wants it. This is emotional incest; a demonic bond between a narcissistic woman and her son.

Mother MADE you.
Mother F*CK you.

CHAPTER 4: Mama's Messy Man-Child

When a toxic narcissistic woman begins to program her little boy, the abuse starts in very subtle ways. Because she is a covert narcissist, she is already spiritually-broken and void of emotion. Sure she can cry like most mothers do, but those tears are crocodile tears. She can falsify her emotions and put on an Emmy-award winning performance when she wants to manipulate anyone on her radar. She is a fraud.

A man that grows up with this type of mother will either witness her Jezebel traits while she is interacting with his own biological father, or either with her multiple "makeshift" boyfriends. She will devote more attention to these abusive men before she caters time and attention to her son. If his biological father is physically abusive and violent towards the whole family, the young boy will lose all respect for his mother for not leaving her abusive marriage with dignity. He will grow up believing that all women have lack of self-respect like his mother. If he observes his mother being promiscuous with multiple men, he will silently resent her and label her a whore. His beliefs will turn into a blanketed disgust for all women.

If his mother is a gossiper and troublemaker (*as all narcissistic women are*), he will indeed pick up those ugly characteristics as he becomes a man. He will subconsciously take on the toxic feminine behaviors that he inherited from being around his narcissistic mother. He "unknowingly" evolves into a woman even though he is still physically a man. He has a love/hate relationship with his mother and this is how he becomes a misogynist. He will also entertain the ideal of sleeping with men on the down low, or come out of the closet as a full blown gay man. His mama is the root cause for his overall hatred of women. He will emulate her gossiping, messy, two-faced behavior. As much as he hates her, the reality is that he acts just like her. This is why you will find out at the end of your relationship that he has been gossiping about you to his mother as well as the other women in his family. He is two-faced like his mother. You will be devastated once you hear about the fucked up rumors and vicious lies that he will spread about you after the break up. Yup, you can blame his mama for teaching him how to run his big mouth like a "Bitch." Real men do not gossip *negatively* to women **ABOUT** other women, nor do they run smear campaigns. That's a feminine characteristic and you should feel uncomfortable being around any man who behaves like this. It's messy and unacceptable. Run.

The whole goal of his demonic mother is to break her little boy down and rebuild him into what she NEEDS him to be in order to satisfy her insecurities. She doesn't give a fuck if she exposes him to abuse. All that matters is that her long term plans to control her son are uninterrupted.

Here are some examples of emasculation by use of different types of abuse tactics that a narcissistic woman will impose on her son in order to control him:

Coddling - This abuse tactic is one where the mother "babies" her son even when he's in the wrong. He is not given consequences when he is supposed to be held accountable for his wrongdoings. If he bullies another child in school, his mother will let him get away with it. If her son disrespects a female, she will defend his abusive behavior and enable him to abuse more females. His behavior is rewarded by his mother instead of reprimanded. She spoils him and tells him that he can do whatever he wants, even when he is wrong. She spoils him and creates a monster. He will expect all women to cater to him financially when he becomes a man, no thanks to his mama.

Verbal abuse – If her baby boy stumbles, hurting his knee, he will most likely cry. His toxic mother will call him a *"Sissy"* or *"Cry Baby"* and tell him to shut his mouth. This is her way of exerting her authoritative power over him as a child. If she's a single parent, she will compare him to his absent father, making him feel worthless as a young man. Her mouth is like a whip. Vicious, thrashing and uncontrollable at all times. She wants her son to know that she wears the skirt AND the pants in the house. Her words break his manhood.

Physical abuse – She uses belts, extension cords, shoes and anything she can get her hands on, to beat her son. He screams in pain as she puts welts all over his body and throws insults at him. The narcissistic mother is enjoying his pain. She is getting off on watching her son squirm in the corner, begging her to stop. He screams every time she slings the belt at him. He urinates in his clothes as his anxiety heightens. Once the beatings are done, she will return hours later to hug and kiss (*coddle*) him. She reinforces her control over her son by explaining to him that she didn't mean to abuse him and that she actually loves him. Yes, even after the name-calling and severe beating, she claims that she loves him. This is not love. This is reinforced intermittence or conditional strengthening of the trauma bond.

The little boy is confused, but because he feels obligated to honor his mother, he convinces himself that her abuse is justified. This creates Cognitive Dissonance in him. He can't even begin to bring himself to leave her even if he wanted to. He knows deep in his heart that his mother is toxic, but he feels too guilty for escaping her grasp. He's stuck. He can't just up and leave his mama. Who will protect her when all of her other men abandon her? So he tolerates the painful whippings for as long as he can. This will continue until the boy becomes strong enough to overpower his mother's physical strength.

Emotional abuse – This type of abuse is silent and covert. It doesn't require physical contact. She is emotionally distant from her son. She's not nurturing or supportive. She's cold and sadistic. She's miserable and constantly projects her misery onto her son. If she is a single mother, she will emotionally neglect her son due to the burden of working multiple jobs. Unfortunately, there is a hefty price that comes with leaving her son behind to fend for himself while she's working. It's called "emotional neglect."

In a single parent home, there is a term called *"Latch Key Kid"* which means that a child has a key to his house and usually has to let himself in once he gets home from school. He has to take care of himself. He has to heat up his own dinner, do his chores and take care of himself because his mother is busy working double shifts. This creates an emotional void in the boy. He is now forced to learn how to survive without the assistance of his mother. He hangs out in the streets while his mother is at work, invites girls into his house for sex while his mother is gone and basically has no structure or boundaries. He is now in survival mode and growing up on his terms due to lack of supervision or consequences.

Mother MADE you.
Mother F*CK you.

CHAPTER 5: Meeting His Narcissistic Mother for the Very First Time

Ah, aren't you the lucky girl? He's bringing you home to meet his mom for the first time. After several dates (and possibly some sex), he feels like you're worthy enough to meet the "other woman" in his life. So you prep for this very special day. You wonder what to wear, how to style your hair. You want to be cute, classy and presentable. Should you buy her some flowers as a nice gesture or bring her some baked cookies? You want to make a really great impression, so you're off to planning your first meet and greet with your future mother-in-law.

You ask him what things does his mother like? You wonder if you have anything in common with her; you wanna be sure to make light conversation and not to say the wrong things to her. You're basically doing your homework before you meet the woman. Honestly, you can do all of the research in the world, but nothing (*and I do mean nothing*) will prepare you for the toxic, narcissistic manipulative web of destruction that lies ahead of you. Unfortunately, your demise has already been carefully plotted very strategically.

So the day is finally here. **THE DAY YOU MEET HIS MOTHER.** He calmly goes down a list of do's and don'ts for you to abide by before you get in front of his mom. He intentionally leaves out the part that his mother is a jealous, fake-Christian who is also a competitive, messy bitch that has basically helped him sabotage all of his past relationships. He doesn't want you to know that part just yet.

You walk through her front door and into her living room; you smell baked chicken all throughout her house. The furniture is old and dated and there are lots of old family photographs hanging in dusty frames all over her walls. She has a China cabinet full of knick knacks and trinkets. She is a hoarder who collects junk. In the corner you will see a giant bag of bingo markers and yarn for her crochet projects. She walks out to greet you with the fakest smile on her face. "Hello _____, my son has told me so much about you!" You reach over to hug her back and she begins to tell you how pretty you are. In the back of her mind, she's sizing you up and calculating how long the relationship will last between you and her son. She asks you what you do for a living and if you have a college degree. She wants to see if you're a witty bitch or a dumb doormat. The smarter and prettier you are, the more of challenge it will be for her to break her son away from you. She's sizing up your potential to steal her man (*I meant your man, lol*) away from her. At the same time, she's also checking your willingness to be used and abused financially.

The task won't be easy, but she's already plotting a scheme to help her son fuck you over.

She's got to play her little acting role and pretend to be this jolly wonderful "Mother-in-Law," laced with Chamomile tea and rose petals. In the back of her mind she's saying: *"**Let the games begin**! **Come over here my dear and sit down at the dinner table. Let me pick your brain because I am threatened by you and your beauty. You are now my competition and I will kill your ass before I allow you to take my son away from me!**"*

Your future mother-in-law will tell you that she's ready for grandkids (*But she won't tell you about the secret babies that her son already has with various women*). She will tell you that she's ready for her son to marry a nice girl like you, but she won't tell you that she wants to live "vicariously" through your marriage in order to keep a close eye on her son. The lies are endless and the smiles are faker than Donald Trump's wispy toupee. You are getting ready to be duped by a toxic tag team duo.

Mother MADE you.
Mother F*CK you.

CHAPTER 6: She's Already Jealous of You

As I discussed in the last chapter, if you're meeting his mother for the first time, she will put on a whole facade. His mama has been through this routine with multiple potential daughter-in-laws, over and over again. She knows her son is a whore, so she doesn't take any of his relationships/situationships seriously. The only time she will be on alert is when he brings a woman of substance with a backbone home to meet her. When his mother sizes you up and realizes that you ain't no immoral hood rat, but rather a Queen with a good job car and a curvy body, you instantly become a threat in her eyes. The challenge will be greater for her to pull the wool over your eyes because she knows that you're not a weak woman.

I hate to be the one to break it to you, but the game is already rigged. The cards are stacked against you from day one. Let me explain. Because his mother is a narcissist, she is deeply insecure. All narcissists are. She is an energy vampire. A liar, manipulator, con artist, whore, gossiper, adulterer, drug and alcohol abuser. Any woman who is the complete opposite of that, is a threat.

When you first meet her, she's looking at your pretty face, your nice clothes, your expensive purse and she sees your nice car parked in front of her house. She automatically goes into competitive mode. She will smile and remain cordial while you're present, however, once you leave, she will begin to plot and scheme how to drive a wedge between you and her son.

Listen to me carefully: YOU ARE A THREAT. If you were to sit down with his mother and interview her about her childhood, you're gonna learn that she is a very weak, broken woman with low self-esteem. She was more than likely abused and/or abandoned during her adolescent years; at some point molested or beaten. She was raised by narcissistic parents, therefore she passed down the abuse to her son. Her insecurities run deep because she was treated like shit and all of her relationships have failed. You have to understand that her son is probably the most loyal man she's ever had, so she will always treat him like her husband.

If a quality woman like yourself comes along and has the potential to clean up her son to make him a better man than what she did, she will compete against you to maintain control over him. If you are strong and have your own opinion and backbone, she will hate you. She is looking to manipulate and take control of your money, time and kindness. If you cannot be used or controlled, she will assist or enable her son by helping him to set up a fling with another woman to drive a wedge between you and him. In other words, she has to play puppet master over her son's relationship in order to feel validated and secure so that he stays under her thumb. The woman that he cheats on you with, already knows his mother and usually is another narcissist that has helped him to break up his past relationships. The side chick sits on the back burner until she is summoned to step in and stir up the drama. His mother is well aware of the plot to destroy you. She is also cool with the sidechick.

Please understand that all of this is calculated and premeditated. You never stood a chance. Narcissists repeat themselves in the same repetitive cycles and their abuse repeats itself with every victim. You're competition to his mother unless you allow her to run all over you and borrow money that she has no intention of paying back. You basically have to become her personal slave to win her over so that she doesn't fear you stealing her son away from her. But you and I already know that ain't gonna work, because you have high standards and you're NOT gonna tolerate his shit or his mother's shit. You're gonna cut both of them off and then they're gonna stalk you to try to pull back into the cycle of abuse again. It's very sick and sadistic.

She knows that you are way above her level. She knows that you are a Queen and she has never conducted herself like one ever. She knows that you are a high achiever and you always accomplish your goals and she feels intimidated by your success. She knows that her son is obsessed with you more than he has been with any other woman. She knows that all of his side chicks are jealous of you. She knows that you're a better quality woman than all of the toxic women in his family. She knows you have the potential to change her son for the better and that may cause him to distance himself from his dysfunctional family. Her jealousy runs deep. Don't take it personal, just block the entire family and move on. You can do so much better. He's gonna be mad when you cut him off when he should really be mad at his mother for raising him to hate women altogether.

Mother MADE you.
Mother F*CK you.

Chapter 7: Her Pussy is More Powerful than Yours

You and your man have LOTS of great sex. Matter of fact, he says you're the best he's ever had. He loves the positions, the comfort, the lust and passion. He loves cuddling with you after he climaxes. You love it too. Your bond is getting stronger and he is idealizing you and strengthening the trauma bond to keep you coming back for more.

During your relationship, you're gonna start noticing that his mother interrupts him more than usual. She will text him sporadically all throughout the day, even while he is at work. Her curiosity will get the best of her, and she will want to keep tabs on her son because she is in secret competition with you. The one advantage you have over her is your good pussy. She can't fuck her son. She understands that there is power in the pussy and it can control a man if wielded the right way. But she will communicate with you indirectly, that her pussy is more powerful than yours. When she is contacting your man and begging him to do favors or lend her money or ask him to stop by her house and fix something, she has a hidden agenda.

It isn't odd for mothers to check in with their sons. However, if she is calling her son numerous times throughout the day on a daily basis, then that is excessive, unnecessary contact. Her insecurities have kicked in and she has to *"insert"* herself into your relationship to show her dominance over you. She has zero respect for your personal boundaries and the unfortunate part of all of this is that your man is too weak to put a stop to her pesky meddling. She never taught her son how to have healthy boundaries because it doesn't benefit her if she cannot control her son. So she can better exert her power over the both of you, if he allows her to overstep his personal boundaries.

This is her way of showing you that her pussy holds more power than yours. Either you fall in line and allow her to control you both, or either suffer the consequences of being cheated on. She won't have it no other way. This is why she stalks her son behind your back and meddles in his personal business. She needs to know how much control your vagina has over him. She needs to know whether or not y'all are planning to run off and elope without her consent. You're a powerful woman. She knew that the moment she laid eyes on you. You can't win her son over unless she's in the middle of everything giving spearheading the instructions. All of the great sex you give him means nothing if he is allowing his mother to dictate the terms of his relationship. And trust me, she will. Good luck with that. She might as well sleep in the bed with y'all.

Mother MADE you.
Mother F*CK you.

CHAPTER 8: Hear No Evil, See No Evil

Since the onslaught of COVID-19 last year, we saw a rise in domestic violence cases across the world. Due to an enforced order for everyone to quarantine indoors, domestic violence victims were forced to stay at home with their abusers. This means that narcissistic sociopaths were inclined to torture their victims at home behind closed doors. The narcissist will always isolate his victim from reaching out to her family or friends for help. He wants to keep his victim trapped and fearful so he can maintain control.

When you are in an abusive relationship with a narcissist, you will always feel alone. You're afraid to disclose the details of your toxic relationship to your friends for fear of being judged. Since you cannot contact your friends or family, you opt to reach out to your in-laws. You figure that these people are the closest thing you have to family and that they present themselves to be loving and supportive. So why not reach out? Wait, not so fast.

What you're going to find out about your toxic mother-in-law is that if you turn to her and confide in her about the domestic violence being committed against you, she will turn a deaf ear and blindly support her abusive son. Unfortunately, she will protect him to no end, even if he disrespects her repeatedly. She doesn't care that she is enabling his aggressive, violent behavior. She doesn't care that he could possibly land himself in jail if he continues to violate innocent women. His mother is right there pretending not to see him in the act. She is going to defend his behavior and project it back onto you. Yes, she will find a reason to blame YOU for him assaulting you.

If you co-parent with him, she will help him fight for full custody over your child. That's right;

she will go to court with him and lie under oath to vilify you as a bad mother to help him win custody. He could beat her in the head with a baseball bat the night before you go to court, she's still gonna show up and help him defeat you. This woman loves abuse. Remember she has taught her son that abuse is normalized behavior in her household. She doesn't give a fuck if he's beating your ass, just as long as he doesn't stray away from her control. You on the other hand, are disposable.

When you learn that your man has been cheating on you, trust me, his mommy already knows. She is cool with the sidechick and has invited the smut into her home behind your back. His mother has zero respect for you and she will help facilitate the love triangle between you, her son and his sidechick. She will help move you out of the picture and break y'all up, just to help him pull in the new whore to replace you. His mommy is all in the middle of her son's love life, helping him to destroy it.

This information is gut wrenching, but I hope it is helping you to understand how narcissistic families move as a cult. They are snake-like and will enable each other's abusive behaviors. They are all predators with his mother as the head ring leader. You never stood a chance in this relationship because it was always set up for you to fail from the very beginning.

The narcissistic mother hears no evil and sees no evil when it comes to her son. By turning the other cheek when her son commits domestic violence, she knows her baby boy will love her more and stay close to her. She picks and chooses sides when it's beneficial to her, so when it comes to her son, she will always choose him over you to keep him close to home. This is how she controls him.

Mother MADE you.
Mother F*CK you.

CHAPTER 9: Christian on Sunday...Demon During the Rest of the Week

One of the things that makes my blood boil are fake Christians. I can't stand a Bitch who thinks she is mightier than you, but she neglects to keep her own household in order. She uses her bible to demonstrate her power over others. Every time she quotes a bible scripture, it's intended to belittle someone into feeling inferior. She's more concerned with her reputation in her fraudulent church community, instead of being an actual woman of God.

One of the ways that so many good women get caught up with narcissistic men and their toxic in-laws, is because they assume that their in-laws are good-hearted, God-fearing Christians. Let me tell you, these low life motherfuckers are the complete opposite. When you first meet his mother, you will witness her attend church on a weekly basis. You are automatically gonna believe that she's a woman with integrity who practices transparency, consistency and clarity as a true Christian would. You want to believe that she has good morals and high standards. Well, this bitch is the total opposite!

Let me tell you something, a narcissistic woman doesn't attend church to become a better woman, rather, she attends church because she needs a place to gossip about others. She needs a refuge to pick up men as well as a place to mask her shitty, toxic behavior. She's more concerned about her reputation because she knows she's a piece of shit behind closed doors.

Going to church helps her hide that filth of a character that she hides from her community oh so well. The church pulpit is her favorite holy place to paint herself innocent and obedient. Once the church service concludes on Sunday, she will switch up her demeanor and go back to being toxic for the remainder of the week. Holy on Sunday, and a messy, money-hungry, manipulative, controlling, fake ass Christian, throughout the rest of the week.

Narcissists do not practice being Christians. They are inconsistent in their morality and behavioral patterns. Abuse and manipulation is what sustains them day-to-day, so practicing and applying Christianity to their daily lives would get in the way of their pathological, destructive behavior.

Actually, narcissists use church to prey on new victims. It's the perfect place where a predator can lurk for the vulnerable, weak people who are looking for an outlet to seek Jesus to help them with their problems. Society teaches us to run to church when we are at our lowest points in our life. We are told to take our addictions and worries to the altar. When we walk through the church doors every Sunday, we are most likely seeking refuge. The narcissists that sit in the congregation are aware of that. They are looking for fresh meat, and church is the perfect place to find it. So you see, church is nothing more than a smoke screen to hide the abusive behaviors of the demonic narcissist.

When his mother is not meddling in his personal business, she is either being a problematic troublemaker to somebody else or either hiding in church. This is all she knows. Where else can she go to hide her filthy, toxic, destructive behavior and make herself look like a saint? Exactly.

When you first meet her, please do not be fooled into thinking that she is a good person, simply because she pretends to be a holy saint who attends Sunday morning worship service every week. Church is nothing more than a cover for manipulators, scammers, pedophiles, adulterers, cheaters, rapists and trash. His mother is all of the above. Get to know her character and don't be fooled by what you see on the outside. Church doesn't mean shit to an abuser. His mother is nothing more than a pig with lipstick on.

Mother MADE you. Mother F*CK you.

Chapter 10: Cacklin' Hens

In most cases, narcissistic men have a tendency to have multiple babymothers. If you find out that your man has a babymama or two waiting in the wing, please beware. He will tell you that his babymama is crazy and bitter just to blow your ego up, but if he's a true narcissist, he is still sleeping with her. Yes, if his babymother is a narcissist as well, she will continue to play the backburner knowing he's involved with you. Narcissists are promiscuous, calculated and trifling. Because his babymother has low self-esteem like his mother, he can play off her insecurities by throwing your relationship in her face to make her jealous. This is called "***Triangulation***" and it works every time on the toxic babymother. This is why she is so eager to help him cheat on the current woman he's supposed to be in a committed relationship with (you). He has slept with his babymother multiple times in all of his other past relationships because she is a willing participant in his toxic love triangle game. The toxic babymother will also work with your narcissistic mother-in-law and sister-in-law to erase you out of the picture.

You have to realize that your in-laws are all narcissists which means they work together like an organized Italian mafia. When one family member abuses an innocent person or does any dirt, the family will work together to sweep the dirt under the rug. If your man assaults you or cheats on you, his family will help him lie and cast you out so that you look like the crazy one. The family can rely on narcissistic babymother to be used as a pawn to join in on the shenanigans.

When you find out that everyone in his family knew you were being cheated on, it will literally break your heart. This is why there are so many similarities between his toxic babymother and his mama. They are literally the same woman, but different age. His babymother is a woman who lacks boundaries, self-respect, self-esteem and standards. She is his secondary mother. His babymama in nothing more than a "surrogate" mommy that he can fuck, use up and groom to become his personal security blanket when he falls out with his biological mother. The relationship he has with his toxic babymother is a very sick, codependent relationship similar to that of his biological mother. The only difference is, he can't fuck his mother.

He can always rely on his toxic babymother to help him bait other women into entangled competitions for his love. The constant love triangles that he and his babymother facilitate against innocent women are exhausting and demonic. Don't play that game with either one of them. They've both been at it for a long time.

His babymother and his mother are one in the same. Even if they bump heads and disagree, they will eventually team up and come against any woman who is a threat to stealing your man away from the family. Narcissists are two-faced and they play both sides of the fence. They can be fighting one minute, and the next minute huddled up, plotting to destroy an innocent person. The premeditated deception is off of the hook. This is why it is imperative to learn about the family dynamic of your in-laws before you sleep with any man.

You must learn his upbringing and whether or not his family are liars and manipulators. His mother will be the ring leader of it all because she is running the whole program. His mother will also use different people as minions/pawns to help maintain control over her son. This is why she will kick it with the babymama or side chick behind your back. It's a dirty game and she thrives off of hurting strong women like you because she's a low life bum. Don't take it personal, just cut the whole family off and never look back. If he wants to keep sleeping with his babymama and running in and out of his mama's house, let him go. Trash belongs with trash. You have better things to do with your life.

To play devil's advocate, all babymamas are not toxic. The narcissistic male also seeks to impregnate empathetic women who have codependency issues. These type of women do not go around helping the narcissist to cheat on other women or willfully allow themselves to be used in the love triangle. They are usually the ones fighting to get away from the narcissist and battling him in family court because his co-parenting skills are counter-productive to the child in common. I'm not speaking about those types of women in this chapter because they really don't know any better. I just want to clarify that.

When I speak about the toxic babymama, I'm specifically talking about the trifling bitches that are narcissistic as well. They are backburner placeholders for the narcissist to use and discard time and time again. These type of women enjoy drama and love interfering in their baby daddy's private love life. They compete with his current girlfriend (you) and any other woman after you. They have no moral compass and will help him to destroy all of his relationships to maintain control over him. If he has more than one babymother, please get out as soon as possible. Even if she doesn't get along with his mother, she will team up with his narcissistic mother if it means going against you. Narcissists are powerless unless they come together as one group. It doesn't matter if they are at odds with each other, Narcissists are notorious for flip-flopping and playing both sides of the fence. If his babymama is toxic, she will fit in perfectly with his already dysfunctional family. You're not built for the dysfunction, so bow out and let Sis have him. He will treat her like shit and she will still remain in the background on standby as the years go on. It's no different than what he saw his mother deal with when it came the toxic men in her own relationships. If his mama lacks self-respect for herself, then he will continue to disrespect her. See the similarities between his mama and his babymama? Birds of a feather will flock together. Cacklin' Hens love drama. I digress.

Mother MADE you.
*Mother F*CK you.*

CHAPTER 11: Playing Both Sides of the Fence

Once you have gotten to know your narcissistic in-laws and have been invited to a few of their events, you should have somewhat of an idea of the dysfunction surrounding the family. As I have mentioned before, narcissists use a manipulation tactic called **"*Triangulation*"** which sparks confrontation between two or more parties. The root of all triangulation is jealousy and gossip.

You will learn in the end, that not only did your significant other partake in triangulating you against his other family members and babymamas, but you'll also learn that his mother was guilty of doing it to you too. What's really gonna blow your mind is that you will come to realize that his mother was playing you against her son the entire time. If you pay attention, you'll notice she'll talk negatively about her son to you to stay on your good side. The reason she does this is because she knows you're a good woman with high standards and she wants you to view her as the same. She knows deep in her heart that she is pure trash and the complete opposite of a high value woman. So in hopes of you respecting her and treating her like a woman of good moral standing, she has to shit on her son to pretend to stay on your good side to sustain your relationship with her. Especially if you're the type of daughter-in-law to lend money, do favors or spend your time being at her beck and call. She enjoys using you for the perks, so she wants to stay on your good side. Unfortunately, she won't be able to sustain this fake relationship with you but for so long, because the bullshit will eventually catch up.

Now on the other hand, when you're not around and she's alone with her son, they are both gonna take turns talking trash about you. That's right, she's gonna entertain her son and every lie he tells her about you. He will run to her and vent about your relationship problems. The rumors are false and created to start more drama amongst your toxic in-laws because he knows that once he tells his mother, she will go above and beyond to tell the rest of his family about your bad behavior. His mother will ensure that the smear campaign against you will spread like wildfire.

She will also smear you to him, then turn around and invite the side chick into her house for dinner. In other words, his mother is going to help him facilitate the destruction of your relationship. She is well aware of all of the cheating and disrespect, however, she must remain on her son's good side to maintain control of her son. So she is going to play both of y'all against each other until you are removed out of the picture when the toxic sidechick/ babymama/ ex-wife/ ex-girlfriend replaces you.

Narcissists love to start fights between two parties. It's the perfect way to incite drama by staging a catfight and disappearing when the war pops off. His mother is guilty of this trifling behavior and it is more than likely that the rest of his family triangulates too. When you find out that you're being thrown into unnecessary drama amongst your in-laws, then it is best to disengage and cut all ties with the entire family (*your ex included*). You have to understand that you are in the middle of a snake pit. The dysfunction in this family runs deep and they have managed to suck you in to it. If you allow them to, they will pull you further down the rabbit hole until you can't pull yourself out of it. They want you to be just as dysfunctional as they are.

If you block them and cut them off, they will turn up their noses at you and treat you as if they kicked you out of their family. They're so delusional that they honestly feel like you're not good enough to be in the family knowing damn well you don't want to be a part of their Jerry Springer shit show. Your morals and their morals do not match, so they pushed you away for not conforming to their bullshit.

Your mother-in-law will be the ring leader facilitating the drama with your man by her side adding fuel to the fire. She has to play both sides of the fence to maintain control of the family's dysfunction. If you don't cooperate you will be discarded like trash unless you remove yourself out of the picture first. Don't take it personal, their dysfunction has nothing to do with how you carry yourself and/or treat people. They're just a bunch of delusional, detached, broken, messy ass fake Christians that love drama. They can't help it, but you can. Get out and stay out.

CHAPTER 12: What If His Mama Is Dead?

When I'm doing my phone coaching sessions with my female clients, it's very common for most of them to complain about their toxic mother-in-law. On the contrary, I also get a lot of women who tell me that their narcissistic husband/ boyfriend/ babyfather do not have a mother because she is deceased. So if there is no mother in the picture, could he still be abusive towards women? How can you research his relationship with his mother if she is no longer living?

Well, where there's smoke, there's usually fire. What I mean is, if your man is a narcissist, then it is more than likely that he comes from a family full of them. If his mama is deceased, there will be another female in the family to presume the surrogate mother role of your man. It's either gonna be his grandmother, sister, auntie, cousin or close friend of the family. In other words, the women in his family are ALL narcissistic and will coddle him the same way that his abusive mother would have if she were still alive. The women in his family are all enablers of abuse and they have a weird sexual, incestuous relationship with your man. It's very inappropriate, but they have normalized this behavior within their family.

This is why it's so important to analyze the moral compass of all of the women in his family because if they are toxic, he will repeat their pathological methods. If you feel uncomfortable around any of the women in his family because they treat your man more like a lover, trust your gut. Anytime a female relative behaves like a lover towards your man, then that is a HUGE red flag. That type of behavior is off limits and you shouldn't tolerate it. Even though his mother is no longer living, the toxic females in his family are going to carry the torch. They will continue to baby him, coddle him, enable his abuse towards innocent women and side with him when he's clearly in the wrong.

So pay attention when you're first meeting his family. If his mama is dead, there will be a "surrogate" mother waiting in the wings to carry out the tradition of the toxic family and that tradition involves hidden secrets of infidelity, incest, molestation, domestic violence, dysfunction and toxicity. These women are jealous, messy enablers. His mother would have treated you the same way if she were alive. Cut them off and don't look back.

Mother MADE you.
Mother F*CK you.

CHAPTER 13: Dating Tips

Tip #1 – On the first few dates, don't be afraid to play detective. Go into the glove compartment of his car during a date and check out the insurance card and registration. Is there a female's name printed on and of the documents? If so, it's safe to say, that it's either his babymother, wife or his mother's name. This is your cue to leave him alone. I don't care what excuse a man will give you, there is no excuse for him to have his shit in another woman's name unless it's his wife. Either way, it's a bad sign. Enjoy the dinner date and never call him back ever again.

Tip #2 – Don't be afraid to ask him about his childhood. Ask him what his relationship was like with his parents growing up. Who is he closer to? His mama or his daddy? If he's closer to his mommy, ask him why? Was he an only child or does he have siblings? If he has siblings, is he the baby that gets special treatment? Is he spoiled by his parents? Does he have self-entitlement issues?

You will find out everything you need to know about him, through his childhood. This will take time, so keep your legs closed and continue to be his friend until you complete your investigation. The more you get him to open up and talk about his childhood, the more you will learn about who he really is. Don't just take his word, but monitor the behavior of his family members. It's very telling.

If he has mental issues or a personality disorder, he must first acknowledge it on his own and seek treatment. Do not diagnose him. He has to do the work to heal himself before he enters into any relationship. That's not your job. You are not his therapist. This is where a lot of women fool themselves into believing that they can save a man that can't be saved. If he's a narcissist, he will die this way. Do not become emotionally attached. The idea is to figure out if he has mental issues on the first few dates; take heed and get the fuck out!

Tip # 3 – How many times does his mother text and call him? Does it seem like he has to "check in" with her quite often to let her know his whereabouts? This is a very bad sign. She should have her own independent life. If you sense that she is clingy and treats her son more like a husband, this is a red flag. Get out.

Tip #4 – Stay off of dating apps. It's dangerous and more women are ending up raped, robbed or murdered on the first date. Enough said.

Tip #5 - If he has multiple babymothers, get out. Unless he's a millionaire like Diddy and can afford to spoil everyone at once, it's not worth it. He can't shower you with affection if his attention is constantly divided by bitter bitches.

Mother MADE you.
Mother F*CK you.

Conclusion

Ladies listen up... It is super critical that you get to know his family before you get in too deep with him. This is a matter of life and death. It can save you a lot of time, money and heartbreak when you do the investigative work. I don't care how well-dressed he is on the first few dates, I don't care if he has a six figure job, I don't care if he graduated from a top Ivy league school... you MUST get to know his mother.

Everything he learns about women is derived from the standards that his mother initially sets before him when he is a child. He will always be attracted to any woman who is like his mother, because he has been subconsciously programmed to connect with narcissistic women who have the same toxic personality traits.

Like I said earlier, of course he will want to be seen with a high quality, good looking woman with a good job and nice car. He will want to brag to his friends and family when he locks down a Queen, however, if he was raised by a piece of shit woman, then he will always downgrade and gravitate towards settling with a hood rat.

He is accustomed to being around women with low self-esteem because that's what his mother has shown him all of his life. He low-key hates her, but he cannot bring himself to cut ties with his mother permanently, so he will continue to take his frustrations out on innocent women for his mother's wrongdoings. It's the way she trained him.

The right man will always put you first (*God first actually*) and he will keep all of the women in his family in check. He won't allow any of his female relatives to disrespect you, gossip about you or make you feel inferior. When the love is real, he will be on top of things to make you feel secure. His actions will show you that he is not only **CONSISTENT** and **TRANSPARENT**, but he also has a high level of respect for you when you're in his presence and when you're not around to defend yourself to his family. A narcissistic man will not only entertain the drama amongst the females in his family, he will also sit up with them and tell vicious lies about you to encourage the division between you and them.

Like I said before, please don't get caught up by the fact that these women have good jobs, degrees and go to church. All of that is a "front" to cover up their piss poor behavior. If their character shows you that they are messy and evil, please believe them the first time around and get the hell out of dodge. You deserve so much better, so bow out gracefully and let your ex obsess over your loss. Had he stepped up his game and cut off his toxic mother, he'd be further in life with an exceptional woman. Queens don't chase behind coddled, weak ass men. That's his mommy's job. Your king is out there looking for you, so stop wasting your time on that fuckboy! His mommy has already ruined him.

Mother MADE you.
Mother F*CK you.

Made in the USA
Las Vegas, NV
11 July 2023